Childhood
Interrupted

A CHILD MIGRANT'S JOURNEY

By Evelyn Donnelly Toms

Childhood Interrupted

A Child Migrant's Journey

By Evelyn Donnelly Toms

This book is dedicated to Juanita and George Wheaton.

I also dedicate this book to Bob, Jane and John and the late Billy, for their lifetime of love and support.

Contents

Introduction

In 1618, a group of orphaned children left Britain for Richmond, Virginia, in the United States of America. It was to be the beginning of an extraordinary era in British History—formerly referred to as The British Child Migration Scheme. This was a more acceptable name to many than Child Separation, and this scheme was to last for more than 350 years.

The final boatload of 90 children left Southampton, England for Australia in 1967. Altogether, about 150,000 children were exported to outposts of the British Empire, including Canada, Australia, New Zealand and to a lesser extent, South Africa, Rhodesia and the Caribbean.

The extraordinary part of this story is that the majority of the British Public had and still have no idea that children were being sent to the Colonies. There was no deliberate plan or official conspiracy to keep it a secret, but there have been some debates and a number of reports and research studies that have been written over the years that indicate that this scheme was never really appreciated by a wide audience.

From the start, child migrants mostly between the ages of four and fourteen were usually rounded up by a Poor Law Guardian or a Representative of the Organization responsible for sending children abroad.

In Canada in the early 1900s, young British children were sent to Canada in the care of voluntary organizations such as Doctor Barnardo's Homes, the Church of England, the Fairbridge Society and the Catholic Council for Overseas Settlement.

You would expect that transported children would be orphans or unwanted street urchins roaming the city, in the way Charles Dickens described them. Child migrants were frequently called orphans because the public's hearts were touched by the plight of orphans and they would be more likely to contribute funds to their welfare. Nevertheless, they were not always orphans. They were far more likely to have been abandoned, illegitimate or from broken or poor homes.

Their parents, when they gave their children up to the care of an institution or society, generally had no idea that the children would end up on the other side of the world. Parents offered children up for adoption but their children were shipped overseas instead, and parents did not know if they would ever see them again. Most parents failed to read the fine print that gave these Societies the right to send the children abroad.

The Organizations sending these children out to distant parts of the Empire were convinced they were doing the children a favour. Some families were seen as failing to provide and these children had only a remote chance of doing well, either financially or due to the effects of war. The Societies worried that if children remained in their homes, they would drift toward the criminal and dangerous classes. So what better reason could there be to send these children to the Colonies to start a better life in a new environment, away from their present inhospitable world?

Unfortunately, when you look more closely at the reasons for Child Migration, less high minded and more pragmatic reasons appear. The cost of maintaining these children in the late 19th century in various institutions was about twelve pounds a year. To send a child overseas cost a one time payment of fifteen pounds. The scheme became a useful way of disposing of unwanted children in a country that was financially challenged. Children in care of a Government Society or Organization had to have the approval of the Secretary of State before being sent overseas. But the children being sent abroad in the care of Voluntary Organizations such as Dr. Barnardo's, Fairbridge, the Church of England or the Catholic Council did not need such approval.

Once children were placed with an Organization, the Organization was responsible for them until the age of majority.

Each Organization made arrangements for a child upon arrival in a new country, but there were no set standards for monitoring the children once they were exported.

Of the many organizations involved in Child Migration, Dr. Barnardo was probably the best known. He was a Londoner who witnessed the waifs and strays in the city with evangelical fervour. He cared about these poor children he intended to send overseas. But these "Home Children" as they were to be called, were brought out in hordes and were often treated with cruelty. This was a dark and shameful time in the Empire's history.

The Catholic Church was involved with Child Migration with no governmental supervision or inspection. The Church sent many children to Rhodesia. There, and in other locations, many children reported sexual abuse by the Christian Brothers.

All Organizations had different strategies but all shared a common thread of transporting "good British stock" throughout the Empire.

The above information was taken from a book written by Phillip Bean and Joy Melville called "Lost Children of the Empire".

"Vision Splendour"

Kingsley Fairbridge was born in Grahamstown, South Africa in 1885. He was the son of a Land Surveyor to the Cape Government, who with his family, moved to Rhodesia.

Young Kingsley Fairbridge went with his father on many surveying expeditions and recognized the emptiness of the Rhodesian bushland.

In 1903, at age 17 years, Kingsley paid a visit to his grandmother in England, and saw, in stark contrast, the big cities with their slums, crowded workhouses and orphanages. He was deeply moved by the thought of children's lives being wasted. After a year, he returned to the underpopulated Rhodesia and began to frame in his mind his "Vision Splendour". To quote in his own words, "I saw great colleges of agriculture, not workhouses springing up in every man—hungry corner of the Empire. I saw children shedding the bondage of bitter circumstances and stretching their legs and minds amid the thousand interests of the farm. I saw waste turn to providence, the waste of unneeded humanity converted to the husbandry of unpeopled acres."

To try to make his vision come true, he decided he must try to win a Rhodes Scholarship, of which he was successful.

In 1909, he addressed a meeting of undergraduates at Oxford University on the subject of Child Migration and that night, the Child Emigration Society was formed. He obtained a diploma in Forestry in 1909 but spent the following two years trying to interest people in his project and raising funds for Child Migration. He married a former nurse, Ruby Ethel Whitmore who had been encouraging and helping him for many years.

In March 1912, the Fairbridge family sailed for Western Australia with a capitol of 2000 pounds, with the Western Australian Government agreeing to pay six pounds for each child's ticket to sail to Australia.

It took several months of frantic clearing of the run down property he had purchased, as well as building basic accommodations for the expected arrival of thirteen boys between the ages of 7 and 13 years. In July 1913, they were followed by a second party of 22 boys. This was the beginning of the Fairbridge Farm School in Pinjarra, Western Australia.

Cottages were built to house the children. A dining hall, a house for his own family and farm buildings were also constructed. He raised 27,000 pounds with the assistance of the Australian Government.

In 1924, Fairbridge died at the young age of 39, weakened by malaria and lymphatic tumours.

And so continued a great work to offer thousands of children a new life and a future of bright promise.

The Fairbridge Society carried on with Kingsley Fairbridge's work and established other farm schools in Australia and Canada to receive more orphans and destitute children.

Information gathered from Wikipedia

Early Days

Much of the following details have been gathered from my Personal File that I was able to obtain from British Social Services in the mid 1980s.

My mother, Henrietta Charlotte Donnelly McCabe was born in North Shields, in the Tynemouth area of North-East England in 1904.

She married John Donnelly in 1927, who died of pneumonia and tuberculosis in March 1934, one month before I was born on April 3, 1934. In 1937, Henrietta married William McCabe who was in the British Army. They lived in North Shields. William McCabe came home on leave and decided to sell the house, leaving my mother and my siblings (half siblings or full siblings, I am not sure) John, Mary, Beatrice and I homeless. He then deserted from the army, which he apparently did three times, and was never seen again.

It is probably around this time that my mother, Henrietta, decided to give up John and Mary to the Fairbridge Society, as it seems, from documentation, that she was financially and psychologically unstable. They most likely were sent to Middlemore Homes, an orphanage, while they awaited their departure to Australia. They ended up at the Fairbridge Farm School in Pinjarra, Western Australia. This was the first school to accept child migrants from Britain.

I have no memories of John and Mary, as I was very young when they left our home.

My other sister Beatrice, my mother and I then moved to 100 Maxwell Street in South Shields, noted for its extreme poverty, high unemployment and crime. The war was raging and the economic conditions were worsening.

Maxwell Street contained a row of joined houses that stretched all the way up the street. We lived in the upstairs part of the house. Even though I was only 7 or 8 years old when I lived there, I recall the "soul less" place. I remember the kitchen very well with a big sideboard and large table and a big open fireplace with a hob for cooking. There didn't seem to be anyone else living there. There were no children nearby to play with. I must have gone to school as I was placed into "Standard 2" when I went to Middlemore Homes, but I have no memories of going to school there.

There were no Christmases or birthdays at Maxwell Street. I had no toys or books. Maxwell Street ran alongside a railway track. I remember walking along the track with another girl and picking up candy wafers (for

KING STREET SOUTH SHIELDS LOOKING EAST.

ice cream sandwiches) that fell off the train. I have no recollection of ever hearing the train whistle.

At the back of the house, there were steps down to the washhouse. This was where my mother would wash our clothes in a big copper cauldron. I think there was a toilet in there. There were bedrooms on the main floor, but I can't remember what they looked like.

Following our move to South Shields, my mother took a position keeping house for a black Seaman named David Saunders. I remember David Saunders and thought that he was a very nice man and he was always kind to me. The fact that he was coloured meant very little to me, but racism was rampant in England at that time and the documentation in my Fairbridge files stresses emphatically that the "atmosphere" I was in was not ideal.

At this point, I was about 7 years old. This is approximately the time my mother applied to the Fairbridge Society for them to take me in.

David Saunders later came to live with my mother and me at 100 Maxwell Street in South Shields, but they did not marry. She always signed her name as Mrs. McCabe. I assume that my mother was still married to William McCabe and as long as she was still his wife, she would receive some of his army pay. He was considered AWOL.

According to my file from Fairbridge my mother's reason for "handing me over" stated that she couldn't find work as long as she had me to look after. She also tried to "hand over" my sister Beatrice at this time, but Fairbridge denied her application because she was too old and in poor health.

I saw very little of Beatrice as she was always away from home to receive medical treatments. I am unsure of the nature of her condition but I do remember her having diphtheria. I have a vague memory of being upstairs with Beatrice writing small letters on paper that said "help us" and throwing them out the window.

David Saunders traveled with the Merchant Navy so he was away for long periods of time. He always came home with exotic gifts for us such as peanut butter, oranges and bananas.

My mother and I made many trips by train to Newcastle to meet with my Fairbridge Society Social Worker, Lillian Coulson. I loved seeing Miss Coulson and enjoyed the trips to her office possibly because of the fact I had no idea why I was being taken there. It was on these trips to Newcastle that I saw many bombed out buildings and I clearly recall the sky being lit up red at night from the fires. The screeching sounds of the air raid sirens were frightening. I remember hearing the dreadful scream of the Doodle Bugs, the unmanned planes that made a screaming sound just before the bombs were dropped, and then the awful thud of the bomb.

I remember the window was blasted out by my bed in our house from the impact of a nearby bomb and my bed was full of broken glass.

I don't remember going to air raid shelters, but Maxwell Street seemed to be largely undamaged by the bombings.

Miss Coulson was a lovely, patient and kind woman who spent her life as a social worker, untangling domestic woes among her clients. My mother, according to Miss Coulson, was a good woman but very difficult to deal with. My mother suffered from depression and some of the documents in my file were signed by psychiatrists. Miss Coulson arranged for me to have some new clothes which Fairbridge would provide, as they kept a supply of used and new clothes in their offices. She also asked my mother to send her my clothes ration coupons that would cover the cost of any extra clothing I needed.

In November 1942, I had a physical examination for acceptance into the Fairbridge Society, and was described by the doctor as "very small, pale but well nourished, tonsils moderately enlarged, tachycardia probably from nerves." Even though I was only 8 years old, I was asked to sign the bottom of the report with my signature to certify that the examination was correct!

Another document signed by a different doctor said, "Having examined Evelyn, it is in my opinion that she is bright and in good health and sound constitution, not suffering from any mental or bodily defect which would prevent her from earning her own living as a domestic."

In another document, I was described as "happy, bright and good tempered." It was at the bottom of this document that my mother then wrote, "I, hereby hand over the child Evelyn Donnelly to the Fairbridge Society." She also gave permission to send me to Australia to join my brother John and sister Mary, but she was advised that sea travel to Australia was too dangerous during the war — so she agreed to send me to Canada.

So, following these examinations, we returned to Maxwell Street to await news that Middlemore Homes, the holding place for children awaiting emigration, would take me.

I was accepted at Middlemore within two months of my application to Fairbridge.

My mother had one more document to sign that read, "I promise to use no influence with a view to remove Evelyn having of my free will placed her in the Society's charge, and indemnify the Society against any claims and demands that may arise in consequence of the child being consequently returned to the Country."

I am quite sure that I was completely unaware of the plans to send me away. Forever. There were no goodbyes and I do not recall crying or making a fuss as I was taken away at night time, possibly by strangers. Perhaps I was sedated, so that I would sleep for the majority of the trip to Middlemore Home.

My mother had already sent two children away, so perhaps she was relieved to see me go. We will never really know…

So, off I went to Middlemore Homes, in Birmingham, England in April 1942.

The document my mother signed to "hand me over"

The Middlemore Days 1942-1943

In 1872, John Middlemore opened several homes for boys and girls, as well as a building that was used as a holding home for children awaiting emigration to the Colonies.

Middlemore Homes had a poor reputation and eventually amalgamated with the Fairbridge Society.

There was serious doubt about how much care was taken to select host farms for the "Home Children" when they were sent abroad. Mr. Middlemore was one of the organizers who sent children to the middle of nowhere where they often suffered terribly. These were city children who were unused to isolation and hard labour in the farmer's fields and barns. These were the "Home Children", many of whom were sent to work in Ontario in the late 19th century as unpaid labourers in freezing cold temperatures with poor accommodations and inadequate nourishment and clothing.

Mr. Middlemore sent these children to these farms and provided no supervision or follow up.

I was on my way to Middlemore Homes in Birmingham. I was about to experience a frightening change in my life that I was not prepared for. I do not recall ever talking to my mother about Fairbridge. How could a mother tell her 8 year old child that she was being sent away from her only home forever? Did I go by train, or was I driven by car? Did I know the person who was escorting me?

I definitely remember arriving at Middlemore.

Middlemore Home in Birmingham, England

Shared bedroom at Middlemore

It was dark when I arrived. I remember seeing a dark, scary brick building. If I had been older and read the novels of Charles Dickens, I would have thought that I had been sent to a Victorian Workhouse!

I was taken into the entryway, which led to a long, dark corridor. It was deathly quiet as it was night time and it was very dimly lit.

I saw a person approach me wearing a long, black dress and a white headdress. She was a nun. I had never met a nun before and I can't remember whether she greeted me or not. She had a scowl on her face and I remember feeling very scared of her. I followed the nun along the dark corridor and noticed a white powder sprinkled along each side of the hallway, and wondered what is was.

The nun led me into the dormitory where all the girls were fast asleep. It was quite dark, lit only by a small light from the doorway. She showed me which bed would be mine, gave me a pair of pyjamas to wear and then she left. I was never asked if I needed to go to the bathroom and it was too dark to look for it, so I spent my first night at Middlemore desperately trying not to wet the bed. I saw the other girls in their beds, but didn't want to wake them so I remained as quiet as I could.

I do remember discovering what that white powder was for. The rows of white powder in the corridor were covered in big, black beetles. The powder must have been a long term treatment to kill the beetles, as it was always there for as long as I stayed at Middlemore. Perhaps it was that disturbing sight that started my lifelong hatred for insects!

The boy's dormitory was apart from the girl's dorm. The only time we saw the boys was at mealtimes and school.

The room where we had our meals was a bright, nice and newer room. This was also where we had activities. I remember a nice woman who was

Shared bathroom at Middlemore

apparently a "playwright". I thought she was going to show us how to "play right". Instead, she taught us how to knit, which we all loved and I ended up being quite a proficient knitter, a skill I used all my life.

I got to know the other girls in time, but made no real attachments. We played outside in a courtyard but were kept separated from the boys. We played hopscotch, skipping and we were nearly always sitting on the cement floor against the brick wall, knitting.

I remember being shocked to see a nun shoving a girl's head into a full sink of water one time. I don't know why she was being punished but I suppose we were all meant to witness the event as a warning! If we did not behave, that would be our fate too.

We did attend school which was separate from Middlemore, located up a long hill that we had to walk up each day. We went to school with children from the local area. It seems odd to me now that we were allowed out of the confines of the home and I wonder how many children ran away.

The only thing I distinctly remember about the school was the day we were in an assembly. It was a large school with many children in attendance. The youngest students, which included me, were sitting on the floor facing the podium which was on the stage. The principal of the school was speaking into the microphone when he suddenly collapsed and apparently died on the spot!

Going to school was the only contact we had with the outside world. How we managed to pass each day I can only guess. Knitting, skipping, eating and sleeping and trying to keep out of mischief were our only occupations. We were left to entertain ourselves. I was at Middlemore for over a year.

It was at this time that I started to write letters to my mother. How I would like to see those letters! Perhaps I wrote these letters because we were told to. I can hardly imaging writing loving letters to my mother, but everyone else was doing it, so I wrote along with them.

In March 1943, I left Middlemore Homes for Benington Place in Hertfordshire. I was more than happy to leave that miserable place staffed with unsympathetic and heartless people.

Happier Times at Benington Place
1943-1945

I arrived at Benington Place in March 1943 with a group of 25 boys and girls. Benington Place was 25 miles north of London.

The moment I arrived, I felt uplifted. At the entrance gates, there was a beautiful, old coach house, perhaps it used to be the Gardener's House. To reach the house we were going to live in, we had to drive down a long tree-lined driveway. It was springtime and the flowers were peeking through the grass. I am sure I had never seen such a beautiful sight!

Benington Place was a large yellow brick country-styled house, with its original foundations dating back to 1630. I was fascinated by the house as it was old, welcoming, warm and pretty. It certainly was a far cry from ugly, old Middlemore. I could hardly wait to go inside. I have always loved old historical houses and enjoyed collecting antiques in my adult years. Perhaps my inspiration came from Benington.

The boys and girls were greeted by Miss Trewick, the Matron, a middle-aged woman with a smiley face and a warm, calm manner.

I just knew I would enjoy living at Benington—and I did! We entered into the Hall, which had a huge oak staircase that divided at the top with a few steps up to the bedrooms and bathrooms. The Hall had an enormous fireplace at one end facing the staircase. The side walls had floor to ceiling windows which let in lots of light.

There were also attic rooms which were probably servants' quarters. The girls' bedrooms was at one end of a long corridor upstairs and the boys' was at the other end. We were never allowed near the boys' end. The girls' bedroom had huge windows looking down on the driveway at the front of the house. There were no dormitories here like Middlemore, where there were 20 beds in each dorm.

The large windows were not locked so we often hung out of them to get a better look at the RAF planes flying overhead.

There were huge, old-fashioned bathrooms on the second floor. The bathtubs must have been Victorian as they were built in and surrounded with mahogany. The toilets were boxed in with the same mahogany.

There was a huge cupboard on the landing that was full of beautiful woollen sweaters—made of New Zealand wool in gorgeous colours. I longed for one of those sweaters, but was not given one to wear!

The house was spotless, but apart from making our own beds, we were not given any chores to do. There must have been a housekeeping staff,

but I don't recall seeing anyone clean or vacuum, perhaps it was all done while we were away at school or playing outside.

The basement of the house was where we ate our meals. I guess the house staff ate there also. I remember the living room well. I particularly loved a big picture of a very colourful parrot with tropical palms in the background. Perhaps it was a souvenir of a tropical holiday that the owners of the house went on. At the far end of the corridor was the kitchen, that was so typical of the older times with a huge Welsh dresser, with big china plates, platters and jugs. The ceiling was full of hooks that held big copper pots. We were not allowed in the kitchen but we could see inside of it on our way to the dining room.

At the other end of the corridor was a room with a door that led to the outside of the house. This room was like a modern day mud room, where you can leave your boots and coats. I remember, on the day we were preparing to leave for Canada, one boy realized he had left his very special soccer shoes behind in this room. He was unable to convince the driver to turn back to get the shoes. Apparently, 60 years later, he went back to

Benington on a tour and wondered if his soccer shoes would still be there. Of course, they weren't there!

On the same level there was a large outdoor patio with tables and chairs. It was there that we ate all our meals in the summer. The only problem with this was that the whole area was swarming with wasps and we had to be careful not to swallow them or be stung. On each table was a jar with a bit of jam in the bottom to trap the wasps. All through our meals, we watched the poor wasps struggle to free themselves. The noise they made was deafening. With the black beetles at Middlemore and the wasps at Benington, I am reminded again why I fear and loathe insects to this day.

Benington stood on a large estate. The property had pretty gardens including a herbaceous border and a huge kitchen garden with fruit trees and vegetables. We were not allowed to enter the kitchen garden, but the gardener would often bring us out a handful of berries to sample. At the back of the house was a huge lawn with a reflection pool.

One day a group of us decided we would clean the pool of all the debris and leaves. So, in we jumped with all our clothes on. We weren't thanked for the effort! Miss Trewick was not pleased that we had ruined our clothes.

The rest of the estate was covered with a thick forest of enormous trees. We spent a good deal of time building forts and eating unripe hazelnuts. The girls made little houses out of logs, boxes and cardboard.

We walked to school each day to a little, brick two-roomed school house, about half a mile to the village. There were two teachers, but Miss Hitchcox was my teacher. She was a bit of a dragon, which was intimidating but she knew how to drill us in the three R's. She would carry a cane as she made us memorize the times tables. We recited these numbers every single day. She taught writing and would not tolerate sloppy work. We all read fluently as she would not tolerate poor literacy.

There was a mobile library that came once a week, since there weren't any books at Benington.

The girls learned embroidery, which I loved. We played outside at recess and we mixed very well with the village children, but they didn't come to Benington and we didn't get invited to their homes. A touch of stigma existed, obviously.

Benington pupils were often late for school. Hertfordshire was not isolated from the war, and many days we were distracted by the sight of German pilots hanging dead in the trees with their parachutes twisted around them. There was even a crashed plane to be seen. We were fascinated by these dead airmen.

Across from the school was a large field where the village country festivals were held.

One of the sights I loved was seeing the bluebells growing in the fields. As far as the eye could see the whole area was blue. The girls couldn't resist picking them even though they didn't survive for long once they were picked. The fields were dazzling with cowslips and buttercups too. I never tired of their beauty.

We heard the air raid sirens when they went off, which we all found frightening. Miss Trewick and her assistant would lead us down to the basement and provide us with hot cocoa and read us stories until it was safe to go upstairs and the "all clear" siren was wailing.

Several Old Fairbridgians (former children who lived in Fairbridge Farm Schools) visited Benington within the last few years. One bit of historical news was interesting. To the right side of the house there is a long linear depression, now partly covered with a tennis court. This is about where the kitchen garden was in my time there. During the 1700s, a Spanish Ambassador had lived in the estate, and had built a large amphitheatre to be used for bull fighting!

The estate has been divided by the new owners. There are now two houses on the estate. The Fairbridge Society had leased the house during the 1940s.

The village where we attended school has also changed. The school house has been renovated to become a private home. The school playground is now a community park.

I can truthfully say that I was happy at Benington. There was such a free and unstructured atmosphere to daily life. We were always outside and active. Miss Trewick was a kind, empathetic woman who ran the place in such a way that made us happy. Discipline did not seem to be a problem. We were all so free to amuse ourselves that we did just that. It was announced in July 1945 that we were all leaving for Canada.

The war was over and the seas were once again safe. As we were all loaded on the bus that would take us to Glasgow, I suddenly realized that I had left my Enid Blyton book in my bedroom. I ran upstairs in time to retrieve the book. When we were all settled and on our way, I opened my book to find that I had accidentally grabbed a copy of the boring, "The Tales of Chaucer"!

We were excited about the voyage to Canada, but I think we were anxious about our new destination that was so far away.

Here I come, Canada!

A New Canadian 1945-1949

Before I detail my trip to Canada, I must explain that by the time I left on the voyage, I had not seen my mother for three years. Interestingly though, there are documents in my file that contain much correspondence from my mother, asking that I come home for a visit with her before I sail. Fairbridge made it quite clear that children taken into their care were not supposed to return home once the application became a legal document. The requests from my mother kept coming to the point that Fairbridge relented only if my mother would finance her own trip to the sailing port.

Letters from my mother came back in anger that since Fairbridge was not willing to pay for her visit, she threatened to write to the Duke of Gloucester as she felt he was "a good man and that he would under stand." Whether the Duke received a letter is doubtful. She was advised by the Fairbridge Society that she could have visited me at Middlemore since I was there for a year. She always had an excuse about costs and her poor health, therefore never coming to visit me there. When I went to Benington Place, she never came to visit me there either, even though I was there for two years.

She had threatened to take me back from Fairbridge as she was "gaining nothing from handing me over to their care." This must have sent up a red flag at Fairbridge so they sent her 34 shillings for her fare and advised her that if she could be at the Central Station Hotel at 8:00 am on Friday July 13, she could see me before I sailed. We were staying there before taking a train to Glasgow where the ship was docked at the Clyde.

Try to imagine an eleven-year-old's reaction to this plan. I obviously had no interest in seeing my mother after three years' apart. Our conductor, Mr. Buckingham, who was responsible for accompanying us on the voyage noted, "Evelyn's mother was not in evidence at the Central Station Hotel. The Agent and I went with Evelyn. We enquired of the

Hotel head porter and scrutinized every face in the Public Rooms. Evelyn didn't seem to be distressed in any way then or since."

I doubt whether I would have recognized her. Even now, I have no recollection of what she looked like. I may have been afraid of confronting her after such a long separation.

Perhaps Fairbridge was relieved that Mrs. McCabe was finally silenced with her demands.

According to the documents, she frequently threatened to take me back. She wrote, "I have not had any benefit with John and Mary, [my half brother and sister whom she handed over years before] it is Fairbridge that will have the gain. If you had helped me to have the bairn return home I would NOT have thought of having her there altogether, but the way I have been treated, this is the way I feel about Fairbridge now. I gave enough when I sent my son and daughter so I am not going to part with anymore as I am going as far as I can to get her back if I have to pay every penny it has cost you to keep her."

My mother thought she had SOLD her children to the Fairbridge Society and expected some compensation. Of course, her continued threats and rantings were ignored.

The Voyage 1945

It was obviously a great adventure to be sailing overseas to Canada, far away from England. It was almost overwhelming to absorb all the interesting things we saw and did on the trip, but the sailing segment was special and unique.

There were ten girls in our party, sailing on the "S.S. ERRIA" The boys sailed on another ship. We left on July 13, 1945, full of anticipation and fear. To be on a big ship with nothing but water around us for almost two weeks was an experience none of us could have imagined. We had shared staterooms and never got tired of looking out of the portholes hoping to be the first to spot land. Owing to the huge responsibility of escorting ten young children, we were restricted to a certain area of the ship where our escort could keep track of us. You can imagine the number of places to explore and get lost in if we had complete freedom of the ship. Our escort kept us busy with crafts, stories and games. It must have been a stressful job. We were all happy, well fed with food we had never tried before like corn on the cob.

There were no mishaps on the trip, and I don't remember anyone developing sea sickness, which I eventually suffered from on voyages later in my life.

We disembarked in Quebec, and after spending a night in a hostel, we then boarded a train to Vancouver. We had regained land legs after the voyage. The train ride must have been chaotic as we girls had joined up with the boys before boarding the train.

We were entranced by the scenery of Canada. Rivers and lakes everywhere. I don't imagine we were given simple chats about the geography we were passing through each day. If not, it was a shame, as the country was huge and the scenery changed every day. We traveled through the forested Ontario and the bare Prairies, where we expected to see cowboys! When we were told we were going to go to Canada, the only thing that aroused our interest was the promise that we would be able to go to school on our own horse!

Vancouver finally came into sight. The boys were frantically trying to identify the automobiles, shouting "There's a Cadillac!" or "There's a Chevrolet!" From Vancouver, we boarded a ferry to Victoria and arrived at the Prince of Wales Fairbridge Farm School in Cowichan Station, near

Duncan on July 29, 1945. This was to be my home for four years. I was just past my 11th birthday.

We were taken to the Fairbridge Farm School by bus and as we passed through the gates, we saw the pretty Chapel with the big clock on the front. We were settled into our cottages, in one side of a duplex. We met our Cottage Mother who was a stern looking, middle-aged woman who showed us no emotion. I do not remember her name.

Life at Fairbridge 1945-1949

The cottages were nice and we were settled into a dormitory with fourteen beds. There was a dining room, where we ate breakfast and Sunday dinners. The cottage mother had her own sitting room which had a fireplace and was quite cozy.

We soon got into a routine of everyday living, which included piling wood beside the fireplace and lighting the Cottage Mother's fire in her sitting room each morning. Once in a while, she would invite us into her sitting room to listen to Lux Theatre, a soap opera, on the radio, which was probably a little too risqué for our innocent ears. She also nearly always had cowboy music on her radio.

As the weeks passed, we became familiar with the cottage life and the rhythm of the school in general, and what was expected of us. This was no Benington, where we had freedom everyday to play outdoors. On Friday, the work schedule was posted. We would search the schedule for our names to see what our jobs were for the upcoming week. The duties were done on Saturday mornings and after school. School had not started yet, as it was summer holidays until September.

The Fairbridge Day School

Every morning at 6:00am, one of us was assigned to get up and go down to the furnace room and light the wood burning furnace, and stack the huge slabs of wood in the furnace room. I remember doing it and being frightened that it would either not light or that I would burn the place down. The furnace was the only source of heat so I presume that once we started school, the Cottage Mother took on the job of keeping it going. To

Class photo 1947 (Me—second row from bottom, second from right)

get up at 6:00am to light the furnace was not only scary, but it was cold and we were still in our pyjamas.

Before we had breakfast in the big dining hall, we all lined up for the Cottage Mother who gave us a tablespoon of cod liver oil. I gagged every time but we had no choice of not swallowing the dreadful stuff.

In line for breakfast, we took turns packing our dishes and cutlery in a basket to haul down to the dining hall and return it after we ate.

The Dining Hall

The dishes were made of stainless steel, just like a prison, I thought. We were responsible for the housekeeping in the cottages every day. Soiled clothes were taken to the laundry and clean clothes returned by the girls who were posted there on the work schedule.

The back yard of our cottages was always piled high with slabs of furnace wood waiting to be stacked.

The Cottage Mother was always on our backs about something. None of the children liked her. I spent a fair amount of time at the woodpile, chopping wood as a punishment for talking back to her. I excelled at talking back, and became a thorn in her side.

Fairbridge Girls preparing for their future—Laundry duty

I was 11 years old when I arrived at the Fairbridge Farm School, and I cannot help but think of my own children at that age who had chores to do, but those chores were age appropriate. At Fairbridge, our duties were hardly chores, but WORK. The work was more than children should be expected to do (such as lighting a furnace and stacking wood!)

It took two of us to carry the baskets of laundry to the farm. Even the Farm Manager felt sorry for us and always rewarded us with cookies or a piece of cake. The major job was polishing the dining hall floor. The dining hall was the size of an Olympic swimming pool. A half dozen of us were assigned to this job. We waxed the floor on our hands and knees, then we polished the floor with "bumpers" which were long handles with a very heavy padding on the end. We swung the bumpers back and forth and we even sang songs while we worked, like a bunch of slaves doing hard labour. This job took most of the morning.

Another job was working in the staff houses or the administrative offices where we cleaned windows and floors. There was no supervision, but I presume this was training for our futures as "domestics", with no one teaching us how to do these jobs.

These jobs I have just written about were jobs for the girls. What the boys had to do, I have no idea, but can imagine that they worked on the farm and in the barns. In pictures of Fairbridge, the boys were always holding lambs, leading a horse or riding a tractor, while pictures of the girls showed them holding brooms, mops and buckets.

From Monday to Sunday, life became a monotonous routine: breakfast, chores, school, chores, dinner and bed—day after day. There seemed to be nothing exciting to look forward to. Our whole existence was within the confines of the farm. It wasn't surprising that apathy was setting in to the children.

The girls would often sing this song that reflected our feelings about Fairbridge life:

Down on Misery Farm

Down on Misery Down on Misery
Down on Misery Farm School Where you work all day
And get no pay

We wax the floors And scrub the doors Down on Misery Down on Misery
Down on Misery Farm School

And gone are the days When I was young and free Now are the days When I work in slavery.

The Koksilah River was in the valley behind the cottages at Fairbridge, and that is where we would swim to cool off and have some fun. I was

Swimming in the Koksilah River

terrified to go in the water, as the boys were constantly jumping on the girls' shoulders and shoving them underwater. It was a nice spot in the summer where we could sit and chat with each other, but there was no supervision and could have resulted in drownings, with the boys' roughness.

I learned to ride a bicycle at Fairbridge.

Since I arrived at Fairbridge in July, we didn't start school for a few months until September, and the kids were very apprehensive about this new experience. The school on the Fairbridge property did not belong to Fairbridge. It was state-run and children who lived in the local area also attended.

Mr. Gillette was the principal of the Fairbridge Day School, and the teachers were all women. Mrs. Gray, a middle-aged woman, was fierce. Any child who misbehaved was put over her knee and spanked in front of the whole class. We had another teacher who was always so miserable that we dreaded her classes.

Mr. Gillette was a young man, probably in his forties, who was extremely strict, especially with the boys. He would not tolerate rowdiness or any bad behaviour. He was known to knock the boys on their heads or pull their ears and haul them out of the class. I actually liked him, especially when he treated us to a recital of "The Cremation of Sam McGee" in French Canadian Patois. I actually loved going to school and managed to complete Grades 3 and 4 in one year and 7 and 8 in another.

We had an annual Sports Day, which we all enjoyed, maybe because we spent the day with the boys. A basketball team was formed and Mr.

My basketball team —Me in centre holding the ball

Gillette was the coach. We won many games with the schoolgirls in Duncan, and even won a trophy.

I was also a member of the church choir at Fairbridge. The Fairbridge Chapel was built in 1938. It was a pretty building that was financed by a donor. Over the years, it has fallen into disrepair. A group of Old Fairbridgians, as well as the members of the Fairbridge Strata that now live on the Fairbridge site today, have raised money to fund the repair.

It is now deemed a Heritage Site. It is well used as a place for weddings and baptisms, as well as church services and concerts.

By the time I was approaching my thirteenth birthday, I felt pretty sick of the bleak, boring, unchallenging and regimented Fairbridge existence. Even the dresses we wore were all the same. The laundry lady was also a

Top: In the church choir (Me–top right) Bottom Right: The Fairbridge Chapel

seamstress and must have bought a MILLION yards of the same material. We all looked identical with no chance of developing any individuality or uniqueness.

My relationship with the Cottage Mother had deteriorated to a level of hatred, and I seemed to revel at the thought of irritating her. It was always said that the Cottage Mother could make or break our lives at Fairbridge. I was an angry young girl in a rebellious stage.

I can't recall why I was sent to the Duties Master, but perhaps I was extra un-cooperative with the Cottage Mother. I arrived at his office not knowing what to expect. I was surprised at how young he seemed. He was blonde and muscular, and told me he was going to give me the strap. I held out my hand and he whacked me several times. Yes, it hurt, but it was my spirit that was being hurt. He could have easily talked to me about why I was behaving this way, but it seemed to me that he was carried away with his position of power. This punishment just made me angrier than ever that a young man would physically hurt a 13-year-old girl.

I used to daydream that I would run away and someone would find me dead in a ditch, and would say "poor Evelyn." I continued to put up with all the things that angered me. I had no choice, as there was no one to listen to my or any other children's problems.

By the time I had turned 14, I was extremely unhappy.

One day in the early summer, I was called into the principal's office and met a woman, Miss Armitage, who wanted to talk to me. I spilled my heart out to her, expressing my deep need to get out of Fairbridge as soon as possible!

Not long after my talk with Miss Armitage, she saw me again to ask how I would feel about being a mother's helper for a couple in Victoria. The job was for Mr. and Mrs. Wheaton, and it was just for the summer, but that sounded great to me. I had no idea that my life was about to change again. Forever.

A New Beginning 1949-1952

Of course, the Fairbridge children were not aware of the imminent closure of the school. Miss Armitage arrived at the school in the spring of 1949. She was probably a social worker that was hired to organize the placement of the children into homes when the school eventually closed. Since I had met her before and she had listened to my concerns, I liked her already. I must have had quite a session with her previously as I had had a "melt down" and told her that I had to get away from Fairbridge as soon as possible to maintain any sort of sanity!

At this time, the couple from Victoria, Mr. and Mrs. George Wheaton had contacted Fairbridge to enquire whether a Fairbridge girl could spend the summer with them and their children as a mother's helper. Mrs. Wheaton was expecting a baby in June of that year.

George and Juanita Wheaton

The Wheaton's were familiar with Fairbridge as they had hired one of the girls several years earlier to help with their two children. Her name was Marjorie Arnison, the future mother of Patricia Skidmore, who has made a name for herself in editing the Fairbridge Gazette, the newsletter for an organization that represents Old Fairbridgians. She has done an amazing job unearthing many facts about Fairbridge in Canada.

Marjorie stayed for a couple of years with the Wheaton family and it was a happy relationship. Pat Skidmore has also written several books about her mother's experiences as a Former Fairbridgian and Child Migrant.

Major Plows, the principal of the whole of the Fairbridge Farm School, of course, had to contact the London office before any decisions were made. I knew nothing about the fact that Miss Armitage had chosen me to go to the Wheaton's if London agreed. The request to allow me to be away from Fairbridge for the summer at the age of 14 was unusual and against their normal policies.

The London office eventually agreed. Major Plows was a kind, empathetic man. He called me into his office and told me that a request had been made for me to go to the Wheaton family. Of course, I jumped at the chance, but I was nervous too, as I had no experience looking after small children or anything else for that matter.

In early July, I arrived at the Wheaton home to a warm welcome, and immediately liked them all. Bob was 9 years old and went to a private school in Victoria. Jane was 5 and had not started school yet. John was the

On our way to church in Mrs. Wheaton's new convertible!

baby, only 1 month old.

Mrs. Wheaton was 34 years old, pretty, intelligent, a great organizer and very energetic. Mr. Wheaton was a handsome, kind man who owned a

Me and my new bicycle—with Jane, Bob and a friend

successful construction company. He worked long hours and had a reputation in Victoria as a man of integrity and was often out of town presenting bids for construction jobs.

Baby John was adorable. I knew I would be happy in their lovely, gracious home. I was not hired help, but would be like a "big sister" who would be included in family activities and treated like part of the family. I shared a pretty pink bedroom with Jane and I bonded with the family. I was finally starting to feel happy again.

At this time, Mr. and Mrs. Wheaton were in the process of building a summer home on Shawnigan Lake. It was a beautiful property and we

Testing out the ice on Shawnigan Lake

were all anxious to see its completion. Mr. and Mrs. Wheaton, Jane and Bob went to check on the building progress almost every weekend, so I was entrusted to look after Baby John, even though I was only 14 years old and had no experience. Mrs. Wheaton taught me how to care for him and I was never afraid to be left alone with him. He was a beautiful, happy baby, and I had plenty of time to attend to my own needs. I loved my new life and all the people in it. It was such a relief to be away from Fairbridge and I thrived in this comfortable environment. This new family life began to erase my anger and bitterness.

Jane and me with our new puppy Missy

I helped with housekeeping and meals, and loved taking John for walks in the lovely, leafy neighbourhoods of Victoria.

As the summer passed, I dreaded returning to Fairbridge. Not being aware of the plans to close the school, I thought I would have to go back to that place in September, as Fairbridge was still responsible for me at 14 years of age.

Mrs. Wheaton was privy to my past history and the two of us had many chats about my mother. She tried to make me understand why my mother had handed me over to Fairbridge. She felt that my mother had a lifestyle that she could not change. I had no sympathy for my mother and sometimes Mrs. Wheaton and I got into some heated discussions, but she tried to convince me that my mother had no other option.

During the late summer, the documents I have proved that Fairbridge was still monitoring my adaptation to the Wheaton family. Of course, all the information confirmed I was happy and Mrs. Wheaton was complimentary about how much I loved being where I was. Time was moving along, and soon I would be back to square one among all the things I deplored.

By the end of August, Mrs. Wheaton approached me and asked if I would consider staying with the family permanently and being enrolled in the local High School. I was deliriously happy and my response, of course was YES! YES! YES!

My Graduation photo from Victoria High School

Mr. and Mrs. Wheaton must have talked about this possibility with each other and Fairbridge. They felt I had the potential to do well in life, starting with going to a regular high school.

The London office had to be in on the plan and it must have caused a bit of chaos as there were many documents about me being offered this unusual opportunity. They wanted to comply with the Fairbridge policies that had been laid down when I became their responsibility. Would I go to church? Would I receive appropriate medical care? What were my responsibilities in the family? Major Plows would have the right to visit me from time to time, and also had the right to remove me from the home if deemed necessary. I would also be receiving visits from the "after care" people in Victoria. I have to give Fairbridge credit for their continued concern over me.

That September, Jane started Kindergarten at St. Margaret's Private School. Bob was still at the Glenlyon Private School and I was registered to start school at Victoria High School.

I loved going to Victoria High School. I made friends quickly, enjoyed the classes and liked the teachers. In the past three months, my life had changed so drastically.

Mr. Wheaton bought me a bicycle to use to get to school and back. To be going to High School in a big city was a huge step for me. Not knowing anyone and going to a school with 1200 students was a bit daunting. The new girls I met and chummed around with often asked me about my family and when I told them I had a foster Mother, I could tell they were curious, but I wasn't about to tell them too much about my past.

I had a boyfriend named Lynn who lived around the corner. I was his date for a formal dance and Mrs. Wheaton took me shopping and bought me a lovely long gown. Lynn's mother didn't appeal to me much. She probably thought I wasn't good enough for her son, as she probably knew where I had come from as she knew the Wheaton Family.

I did not hang around with the girls after school who stopped at the drug store to peruse movie magazines and drink Coca Cola. Instead, I had to get home to take John for a walk or stay with the children while Mrs. Wheaton did her errands. I used to come home for lunch which was always a treat—delicious home made soup, made by a woman who came to the house to clean and do some cooking.

I joined the field hockey team and became a member of the C.G.I.T. (Canadian Girls in Training). We often helped out at concerts and school events. I felt like a CANADIAN girl at last.

All in all, the four years at Victoria High School flew by, and I managed to make it to the Honour Roll.

The Closure of the Prince of Wales Fairbridge Farm School

In 1935, the 416 hectare Pemberlea Farm, in Cowichan Station, near Duncan, B.C. was purchased by the Fairbridge Society and was named the Prince of Wales Fairbridge Farm School. Construction began of four cottages, the main kitchen and cook's cottage.

The first party of 17 boys and 14 girls arrived at the school in 1936. The second party of 13 girls and 16 boys arrived in 1936. More cottages had to be constructed. Throughout 1937 to 1938, more buildings, such as staff housing, were constructed such as staff housing. Mr W.J. Logan was the principal.

The children kept arriving until 1941 when the immigration stopped until after the war. Child migration recommenced in July 1945, when my ship sailed to Canada. The last group arrived in May 1948 bringing the total to 327 children who called the Prince of Wales Fairbridge Farm School their home.

In 1949, it was decided that no additional children would be coming from Britain.

The financial support to Fairbridge was almost impossible as Britain was in terrible economic times. Also, methods of caring for poor children were changing, so the decision was made to close the school.

All the Fairbridge Farm prize-winning livestock and machinery were auctioned off in December 1949. In 1952, the children at the school were placed with suitable families in the area.

The final sale of the property took place in January 1975 to Bellamy Property. The Fairbridge Village site was retained as a residential neighbourhood, subdivided into 57-foot lots, managed by a Strata. The first Fairbridge Strata Council was formed on March 2, 1987.

The cottages and offices remain as homes today, but the school, dining hall and hospital were demolished. The Fairbridge Chapel was designated a Heritage Site, and is supported financially by the Fairbridge Chapel Heritage Society and by private donations.

The Years Following
1953-present

Jane likes to call me Miss Grateful, and she is right. I am extremely grateful for the opportunities in my life that came about when the Wheaton family enfolded me with love and guidance. I am connected to the Wheaton family with love, not blood. Did I happen to be in the wrong place at the right time, when George and Juanita Wheaton took me under their wing?

The Wheaton Family taught me so much that Fairbridge couldn't.

I am grateful that Fairbridge exported me to a country where I could fulfil my dreams. But Fairbridge, in my opinion, was a misguided venture. They did their best in many ways but I consider the four years I spent at Fairbridge to be damaging and unhappy.

The girls especially, were just warehoused, while their expectations only guaranteed working as domestic help. My mother was at that stage already when I left for Fairbridge!

As a result of being given the opportunity to go to High School, I was eligible to pursue becoming a nurse, a profession that enabled me to become independent and self sufficient.

I always dreamed of becoming a nurse, and when I reached that point, I was very proud of my accomplishments. I often wondered if I could have

Me as a Probationary Nurse

reached that goal without the support of the Wheaton family. At my Nursing Graduation, I was given the award for "The Greatest Promise of Professional Development". Juanita taught me so much, including how to cook, how to keep an organized home, how to look nice and how to be nice, and also how to laugh. I think she taught me the same things that she taught her own children. However, she could never convince me to jump off the boathouse into Shawnigan Lake!

In the three years I trained for nursing at the Royal Jubilee Hospital, I went home on holidays and weekends and I was always part of family events such as birthdays and Christmas. At this time, Juanita had another child named Billy. He was a bright, sweet addition to the family and I looked forward to visiting him when I came home to visit. Sadly, Billy died as a result of a climbing accident at the age of 17.

After I graduated from Nurse's Training in 1955, I felt fully prepared to make my own decisions about my future. I traveled to Europe with my good friend Liz Williams, who was a nurse at the Royal Jubilee Hospital too. We worked together in the delivery room. While on that trip, I had the idea of looking up my mother, but when I inquired about the whereabouts of 100 Maxwell Street, I was told that the homes were all gone and had been redeveloped. I was relieved to hear that news. I had not been too interested in the possibility of reuniting with my mother, so that put an end to my curiosity.

Juanita jumping off the boathouse at Shawnigan Lake

The next trip I took was to Australia, which also helped to settle my curiosity about my half brother and sister, John and Mary. I have to say that upon meeting them, I liked them well enough, but felt no real connection to them. I never kept in touch.

It was during these travels that I happened to meet a nice man from Toronto named Donald Toms who later became my husband!

Don and I in Australia 1962   *Our wedding day*

This romance distracted me to leave Australia and head to New Zealand where Don had taken a job. We spent time together there and then returned home to Victoria. Later that year, I traveled back to England, to meet up with fellow travellers as well as Don from my trip to Australia and we both returned to Canada together.

I relocated to Toronto and moved into a house with girlfriends, and was able to be close to Don and think about our future together. We married on June 27, 1964. Jane was one of my bridesmaids and John, at the age of 16, gave me away.

On August 24, 1965, our son Christopher was born and on October 12, 1968, Kathryn was born. I stayed home from work to look after the children until they were old enough to care for themselves.

Our family continues to have wonderful experiences with the Wheatons, experiences I would never have dreamed of. George and Juanita also had a vacation home on Grand Cayman Island for many years, where we spent several holidays.

In 1972, Don was transferred for his job with Searle Canada to Edmonton. We lived there for three years.

Kathryn and Christopher—1968

Being closer to the west, we were able to spend more time with the Wheatons at their beautiful summer home at Shawnigan Lake.

In 1980, George unexpectedly passed away from cancer at the age of 69. It was devastating news for all of us but Juanita carried on in her usual strong way. We were living in Oakville, Ontario again by this time, having moved back from Edmonton.

The view of Shawnigan Lake from the porch

The children were well established into their teenage years so I made the decision to go back to work, nursing at the Oakville Trafalgar Hospital.

I loved my job and it was a good decision to go back. I made many new friends with the nurses, whom I still consider close friends today.

Christopher went to Sheridan College in Oakville to study Business and Kathryn attended McMaster University in Hamilton to earn a degree in Sociology and then went on to Humber College for her Certification in Human Resources.

Having moved back to Oakville, I had also made friends with people not connected to nursing, like Mary Clarke, Rosemary Simmons and Elena Barrington, and Ellen Hawkins, and to this day they remain my best friends. They were all so kind and supportive when Don died too young in 1997 of cancer, one year after he retired at the age of 61.

Don lived long enough to be present for Christopher's marriage to Fiona McQuade. They were married in Scotland with all the trimmings of kilts and bagpipes. Juanita traveled with us to Scotland for the wedding and we were able to enjoy some sightseeing for a few days afterwards. Since she was a Cameron, she loved cultivating her Scottish roots.

In 1996, six months before Don's death, he walked Kathryn down the aisle to marry Kevin Adams, an officer with the Ontario Provincial Police. The wedding took place in Oakville and the whole Wheaton family attended.

Top: Kevin, Me, Kathryn, Bottom: Christopher, Fiona

My Grandchildren—Iain, Andrew, Cameron and Meagan

Kathryn and Christopher have both been successful in their careers, are happily married and each have two remarkable children. I am a grandmother to Andrew, Iain, Meagan and Cameron.

Juanita then married a wonderful man, Joe Tully who was a cousin of George's. No one could hug like Joe! They had thirteen wonderful years together, travelling all over the world before he passed away about ten years ago.

I loved Juanita's mother, Helene (we all called her Gram) with all my heart. Everyone loved Gram. She was beautiful, young at heart and delightful to be around. Juanita used to ask her to stay with me and the children when she and George went away. We laughed and giggled the whole time and the children loved her too.

Peter and Jane Powell

She died at the age of 105 and we all miss her so much, especially Jane who had a loving close relationship with her.

Jane married Peter Powell and had a daughter named Katie (Jane and I both fought over the name Kathryn/Katharine for any future daughters, so we compromised!)

John and Kim Wheaton

Jane and Peter built a beautiful home in Washington State, on a ranch alongside acres of federal land and trails. The kids learned to ride their horses and are famous for crying their eyeballs out when it is time to say goodbye. Jane shines with her fantastic meals, especially the cowboy breakfasts. Peter drives us to town in one of his antique cars.

John and Kim live in Moses Lake, Washington. John is a well known Orthopaedic Surgeon and Kim is an accomplished artist. They have four children, Poppy, Laura, Will and Henry.

Bob and Julie live in Victoria, B.C. and have three children, Fraser, Spencer and Ashley. The boys live in Calgary and Ashley lives in Vancouver.

Poppy lives in Portland, Oregon with her husband Tim Bernasek, and their two children, Audrey and Thomas. They live near Juanita, who now lives in an Assisted Living facility in Portland, so they can keep an eye on her. They are so good to Juanita, and the kids are lucky to be so close by. Juanita feels that she is the oldest person living there but I bet she is the "youngest at heart". Jane and Peter's daughter Katie also earned a nursing

Bob and Julie Wheaton

degree. She currently runs a pet care company but also does phlebotomy at a local hospital. Katie and I share our love for cats so we often chat on the phone and compare cat stories. She lives in Seattle, Washington.

Katie was always fascinated with my story and the fact that she had finally met a "real orphan" like the one she saw in the play, "Little Orphan Annie."

I remain very close to Jane, and she and Katie keep me up to date on family news. Jane is a real sister to me and always has been and always will be. I live in Oakville in an attractive condominium. Many of my friends here have met Juanita and loved her the minute they met her. They are so pleased to learn of her upcoming 100th birthday (February 28, 2014)

We are all heading to Victoria this summer (July 2014) for a big party to celebrate Juanita's 100th birthday!

Love

Juanita has always been a mother to me and this memoir is a tribute to her and all the Wheaton family.

Jane and I were helping Juanita move from Victoria to live at Shawnigan Lake, when we found a scrap of paper with some writing on it.

The note said, "Today, I am with my beloved daughter, Evelyn, who is not from my womb, but from my heart. She came to me from Fairbridge Farm School when she was 14, to help mind my children. She has never left me, and I am forever grateful and fortunate for that."

IF THAT ISN'T LOVE, THEN WHAT IS?

The End

Juanita (R.I.P 1914-2020)

The Chapter Afterwards

Written by Kathryn Adams
daughter of Evelyn Donnelly Toms

The writing of my mom's book was an enormous accomplishment after years of thinking about it, talking about it, and wondering where to start. After months of revisions and editing, it was ready to print with the help of a few people that knew the best way to go about it.

When the book was printed, and the copies were mailed home, the pride my mom felt was obvious. The pride I felt was immense!!! She was an author!

As I helped to edit her book, I learned so much about my mom's life, when I thought I knew most of it already.

The completion of this book coincided with the event of my Grandmother, Juanita Wheaton's 100th birthday, and a huge party was planned at Shawnigan Lake, BC for July 26, 2014 to celebrate. It was decided that my mom would dedicate the book to my Grandma and present it to her for her birthday. The sad truth to this is that my Grandmother is in the advanced stages of Alzheimer's Disease, so she would probably be unable to read and understand the words my mom had written.

I came up with the idea to have a "Book Signing Party" with the family, since this was to be an event where most of the family members were going to be gathered together. We could really make a big deal about it. I had a big sign made up that looked liked something you would see at a professional book signing, with a picture of the book, "fake" reviews on it, and a date to come and see the Author. We had champagne and many copies of the book available for people to see and to give to certain members of the family to keep.

I knew my mom was nervous to present the book and open herself up to the emotions held inside for so long, and I know she was anxious for people to like what she wrote and think she did a good job. She stood up in front of the whole family, choking back nerves and tears and spoke about how she was the luckiest girl in the world to have been taken in by the Wheaton's and made a part of the family. My mom drew everyone's attention to the inscription in the front dedicating the book to Juanita. Even with Alzheimer's, my Grandma knew and remembered my mom's story, and was deeply touched by this occasion.

Following a wonderful party to celebrate my Grandma's 100th birthday, we planned a visit to The Fairbridge Farm School in Cowichan Station together. I had been there before when I was 13 years old, but here was the opportunity for my children to visit this place they had heard and read about.

My mom had not been there for years, but when we arrived, the first thing we noticed was a sign with a list of names of children who had lived at the farm and we found my mom's name!! We walked around the beautiful old church, took tons of pictures and found the same cottage that my mom lived in as a girl. It is a treasured memory for me to have had us all there, after the book had been written and being able to see in person where my mom lived when she first arrived in Canada.

After we returned from our holiday in British Columbia, I had been thinking a lot about our trip and the memories we uncovered about my mom's life. I had been toying with the idea of asking her if she would ever be interested in traveling to England to go back to South Shields, where she was born. I gently planted the idea and let it simmer with her for awhile. The next thing I knew, we were planning a trip to England!!

We decided we would go to England in April of 2015. This gave us several months to save, plan and get ready. At this point, I had already begun some research into my mom's family tree. With some additional help from researchers, and Facebook, I was able to find several family members still living in South Shields. A chance reply to an inquiry made on Facebook resulted in obtaining the phone number of a first cousin, my mom's sister Beatrice's son. His name was John Richardson. I called the number and had a very happy, friendly conversation with John and his wife Marjorie. I learned that he had a daughter named Kathryn. The fact that her name was spelled the same as mine was a really interesting coincidence! They were thrilled to hear from me, had always known of my mom and were more than happy to welcome us to their home while visiting South Shields.

During our conversation, I also asked them if they had any photographs of my mother's mother, Henrietta (who they called Lottie - short for her

middle name Charlotte). They assured me that they would find some photos for us, and that they would love to have us to their home for lunch.

In the meantime, we were able to locate Henrietta's grave, in the Harton Cemetery in South Shields. We learned that she died in 1977 of cervical cancer and was buried beside her husband David Saunders who died in 1966. Their graves were unmarked. It had always been a distant dream of mine to find her some day, and was amazed to learn that she actually lived until 1977. I imagined that she had died during a bombing raid in the war, or something equally tragic.

We also learned that my mom's sister Beatrice had died in 1988 of lung cancer and was buried in the Hebburn Cemetery in the village of Hebburn, near South Shields. My mom always remembered Beatrice as being sickly, so I was also amazed that she lived a fairly long life.

In researching the family tree, I was able to learn that Beatrice went on to have 4 children: David, John, Caroline and Reefath (all Richardson-except for David, her first child)

From what I learned, Beatrice got pregnant with David in 1945, and the baby was largely raised by Lottie, and was treated like her own son. He was given the surname Saunders, not Donnelly. Then Beatrice married Oliver Richardson and had John, Caroline and Reefath.

It wasn't until I spoke with John and Marjorie that I learned that Caroline lives in Herisau, Switzerland with her husband and two sons, Stephan and Samuel.

Sadly, Reefath passed away in 2011 from lung cancer. He was only 55 years old. He had two sons Alan and Philip, apparently adopted, but I have not been able to confirm this.

When my mom and I first decided to travel to England, I had the idea to take us to visit Highclere Castle, which is where they film the TV show Downton Abbey. We both love that program and it is filmed at a gorgeous old mansion not far from London. We booked two seats on a tour bus before we even bought our plane tickets to England!

We left Toronto on a night flight to London. We arrived the next morning at Heathrow and had to take a 50 minute Tube ride to our hotel. I had chosen a hotel in the Bloomsbury district of London, right next to the British Museum because I had stayed there when I went to London after university, and loved it. It was walkable, near the Tube, safe and familiar.

We walked from the Tube station to our hotel, a pretty Boutique hotel called The Montague on the Gardens. Our room was teeny-tiny but very cute and clean! We were exhausted so we had a nap, woke up and felt well enough to look for some dinner. We found a cool and busy pub to get a feed of English fish and chips as well as a cold gin and tonic.

It was heavenly. And fun.

We slept well that night and were excited to explore the city a bit the next day. Careful not to expect mom to walk too many miles, we hopped onto the Tube and headed to Selfridges and shopping on Oxford Street. We had fun wandering through the huge department store, picking up a few odds and ends. Mom wanted to pop into Marks & Spencer's to get some of their infamous underpants, so that is what we did!

We hopped back onto the Tube and headed to Westminster Abbey. When we exited the Tube Station, what a sight!! The sun was setting, and left a glow on the big shiny clock, Big Ben! It actually took us a few minutes to realize that that big clock was actually BIG BEN! We sat in a nearby park and took in the sights while we listened to the chimes. The Abbey was closed but that was fine with us.

Since our hotel was literally right next door to the British Museum, we could not pass on the opportunity to see the Rosetta Stone, an Easter Island Man and many other priceless pieces in the museum. Admission to The British Museum is free so that was a surprise.

The next day was DOWNTON DAY!

We had to be up early for our tour of Highclere Castle and the Cotswolds. We had booked two tickets on a lovely bus with the most amazing tour guide, Andrew. He was born and raised in Oxford, was very smart and knowledgeable about all things Downton, as well as the Cotswolds. The bus ride from London took an hour. After visiting two small, quaint unmodernized villages used as filming sites for the show, we stopped at a small church with an amazing old cemetery attached. After those short stops, it was on to the Castle!

The visit to Highclere Castle was extraordinary!!! The sun was shining and we loved walking through the incredible house and were fortunate enough to have a long chat with Lady Fiona Carvarnon - the Countess of Highclere Castle! We snuck photographs of the house as photography was forbidden - but how could we not? That staircase!!! We had tea in the

tearoom and bought souvenirs. The grounds were gorgeous and we almost had the place to ourselves as it wasn't very busy.

We were so happy with our tour, and at the end of the day we were dropped off almost at the front door of our hotel. Back to the pub for dinner and then to bed.

The next day, we took a commuter train to Stevenage, which was about 30 minutes north of London. Stevenage is the closest train stop to Benington.

During our preparations for the trip and to learn more about my mom's English experiences, I spent about six months trying to locate Benington, a large English country house that my mom lived in for a year prior to being sent to Canada with the Fairbridge Association. This house was rented by Fairbridge as a holding home for the children before they were to be emigrated. My mom loved living there. She would describe life there as being fairly free, running around the property, where she saw flowers blooming for the first time. In the spring, the whole property would be blooming with bluebells.

I happened upon a Google Search of a man who had recently renovated his home in Benington, Hertfordshire. His name was Marcus Taverner. The house sounded very like the one my mom described. I searched for a Marcus Taverner in Benington and found him to be a London Barrister. His email address was listed so I took the chance and sent him a quick message asking him if he was the owner of this home that at one time housed children with Fairbridge. He answered me within an hour, saying that, yes, he most certainly did live in that house and we were welcome to visit anytime - just name the date!

I was so excited to make this discovery and found the location on the map, and set to making a reservation at a nearby bed and breakfast for a quick visit to Benington.

A taxi took us to the MOST AMAZING 300 year old thatched roof cottage, bed and breakfast in Benington. We were greeted by two big dogs, and were shown our two rooms, the only nights we would spend apart during the trip. The cottage was breathtaking, and so quintessentially English.

We had made arrangements to visit Benington House that afternoon, so we wandered down the same road my mother would have taken to walk to school each day, towards the big house. I already knew exactly where it would be, but I challenged my mom to see if she could find it as we would be walking right by the house.

She recognized the small cottage at the end of a long laneway right away! She had always admired this little cottage, that at one time might have been a caretakers cottage, but the children at Benington were never allowed to go inside. Apparently someone lives in that little cottage today.

When we arrived at Benington, Marcus Taverner's wife Debbie greeted us. She invited us in and it didn't take long for my mom to recognize several features of the house. Don't forget, she had only been 8 years old when she was last here. She was now 81 years old!

Debbie invited us to have some tea, along with her daughter, who was attending university to become a nurse. Debbie showed us her collection of Fairbridge information that she has collected over the years.

Apparently 12 former Fairbridge children have been back to visit the house in the past 20 years. They are proud to open their home to these children, especially since these children all had such lovely memories of living there. I was so happy when she expressed her pride in maintaining the legacy of this home, and was keeping that legacy alive by allowing people to visit and share in their trip down memory lane.

She took us upstairs to what would have been my mother's bedroom. We passed the bathroom which my mom remembered well. The same wooden built-in bathtub was STILL THERE! The bedroom was also basically the same. It was large with huge windows that looked over the garden. She also took us up to the attic, where my mom remembered spending two weeks recuperating from the Mumps. Apparently the attic was a sort of Infirmary, but today it is largely unfinished, as Debbie and Marcus planned to renovate it as a recreation area for their children but never finished it.

The house was breathtaking. An obviously extensive renovation had been done on the house as Debbie told us they bought the house in very run down condition. Half of the roof had been missing and a lot of moisture had done damage. They put in a large swimming pool with a large piece of garden art around the yard. She showed us two ancient urns that had been dug up when they put in the swimming pool and did some research to find that they were VERY old.

Debbie then allowed the two of us to just wander the property and enjoy ourselves. It was the highlight of the trip overall, my mom told me when we got back from England. When we were ready to go, Debbie offered to drive us back to our Bed and Breakfast, and was gracious to offer to drive us around the village a little bit. She took us to the little school my mom attended while living in Benington. My mom recognized it - a small brick building attached to a church with unique flint stone decorations on the walls. She also pointed out the village green where my mom had attended fairs and parties. It was such an idyllic pretty little place, a village that has now become a commuter town on the outskirts of London. Homes there are very expensive.

We ate dinner that night in a spectacular 400 year old pub called The Bull in Watton-on-Stone, a nearby village with a wonderful pub. The Gin and Tonic tasted very sweet that night!

We were having such a great time.

Our next stop was to visit The Child Migrants Trust offices in Nottingham, they had been helpful with finding Lottie's grave and obtaining other files from my mom's time with Fairbridge. We arranged to stay in a hotel for the night on our way north towards Newcastle and South Shields.

We took the train from Stevenage to Nottingham, a working class town in central England, but were excited to see the Tudor architecture most noted from the story of Robin Hood. We checked in to our hotel and wandered around to see the big castle and old streets. We watched children play in a large fountain in the centre of town, as it was an unusually warm

April day in England. We were tired that night so didn't really do much but relax and go to sleep.

The next morning, we took a taxi to the Child Migrants Trust offices, where we met Lindsey Hughes, a social worker that worked there. She served us tea and treats while we looked at interesting photographs of Fairbridge and other migrant children and my mom told us memories of her experiences. This Trust helps children reconnect with lost family members and works to raise awareness of British Child Migration.

The Trust is located in a cozy, century home with a big comfortable room for meetings. We were unfortunate to not be able to personally meet the founder of the Trust, Margaret Humphreys, as she was in Australia at that time, attending hearings on abuse in the homes of many British Child Migrants. She is a real champion in raising awareness of the difficulties Britain placed on the children who were given up and migrated all over the world.

Lindsey gave us a copy of Margaret's book, "Oranges and Sunshine" which was made into a movie that my mom and I had already seen. It is a well written and very informative book on the subject. You can't help but think this book was written largely about many of my mother's personal experiences. This was a very worthwhile visit.

After our meeting, Lindsey drove us to the train station, where we boarded a train headed for York, a place I had always wanted to visit. My mom had been there before, on her trip to England in 1959!

In York, we had booked a hotel room in the historic Royal York Hotel. It is located right next to the train station and is where wealthy businessmen would stay during their visits to York. It was a short walk to the gorgeous York Minster, that is famous for its immense and beautiful stained glass windows.

We wandered through the old streets that looked like they were from the pages of a magazine. I must also note that the entire time we had been in England, the sky was clear and blue, not a cloud to be seen. How lucky were we? We found a quaint place to eat dinner and enjoyed Steak Frites and of course, a Gin and Tonic. We slept well that night in our huge room at the Royal York Hotel.

Now, at this point, we were getting ready to head north again, on the train to Newcastle, where we would then take a small commuter train to South Shields. I was starting to get butterflies in my stomach, as I was nervous and hopeful that my mom would embrace this time and share in my excitement to see where she had come from. Writing her book and taking this trip had brought a lot of memories back to the surface for her.

We hopped on the train to Newcastle from York, and "accidentally" sat in the first class car. The conductor noticed that we did not have first class tickets, but since there were so many empty seats he said it was fine for us to stay there. Out the windows, we could see beautiful rolling hills, the Durham Castle and then finally the city of Newcastle. My mom could remember taking the train there as a girl with her mother. The train station is a classic old English station, with lots of character and detail.

We found the METRO station with the trains to South Shields, bought our tickets from a little vending machine and boarded. We were finally going to see this place I had always wondered about.

When we arrived, I planned for us to walk to our hotel, which wasn't very far. With our suitcases dragging behind us, it was a longer walk than planned and we were tired. Leaving the train station, the first thing my mom saw was a florist shop. She said, "Well, we'd better get some flowers for my mothers grave". I was stunned and so happy!!! We walked across the street, ordered three white roses and asked the shop keeper to tie them together with a ribbon.

I had thought about doing this myself but was trying to be sensitive to my mom's feelings and didn't want to make too big a deal about visiting her mother's grave.

With flowers in hand, we headed to the hotel. We had booked into a cute, historic hotel called The Sir William Fox Inn, in the Westoe area. It was a pretty part of town, with big old houses that once belonged to the shipping magnates and coal mine owners. (all those businesses are now gone) The hotel was quaint and quiet. We had a nice room with two twin beds. We were pretty tired, and mom wanted a rest, but I was dying to see

South Shields so I went for a stroll by myself down the road. There were rows and rows of terraced houses, mostly brick or stone, until I actually reached a road that viewed the sea. It was a cute town, I felt nervous and excited at the same time.

I had done so much research about South Shields before we left, that I felt like I could have walked all over town without a map. There was so much that I wanted to show my mom. But first, I had to call my cousins John and Marjorie to let them know we had arrived and to figure out when we would meet for lunch. We would just enjoy our time in South Shields around that visit. They were happy to hear from me and invited us to lunch the next day at 1:00. I had also made arrangements to take my mom for a tour of the South Shields town hall with a woman I had met online, who was a town councillor. How amazing is that?

We slept well and had a good breakfast in the morning. Our plan was to go to the Harton Cemetery, where my mom's mother was buried. The cemetery was only about a twenty minute walk from the hotel, so with roses in hand, off we went. I was shaking. We knew the burial plot was unmarked, but that didn't matter to me. I knew exactly where it was. The fact that we were going to pay our respects to my mom's mother, who in an act of kindness, or whatever, gave my mother up to Fairbridge who brought her to Canada, meant that I could "thank" her. My mom admitted that she did not plan to "say anything" to her mother,'s grave which was totally alright with me. I was still overjoyed that she was at the very least, coming to the cemetery with me.

The Harton Cemetery is huge and OLD, and very unkept. Many of the old English cemeteries are not well maintained, but to me, this made it look even more impressive. There were hundreds of large, leaning stones everywhere, many beautiful trees and a pretty chapel stood in the centre of the cemetery.

I had studied the cemetery map, and had a good idea where the plot was, but just to be sure, we asked three young cemetery workers for some direction. They found the plot number, and pointed us to a large grassy spot in the cemetery that held the remains of Henrietta Charlotte Chatman Jackson Hoult Donnelly and her third husband David Saunders. We thanked the men and they left us alone. We stood there for a minute or two, and then my mom bent down, laid the roses on the ground and said, "well, I haven't forgotten about you". I said nothing, but just took in the magnitude of this moment, not just to me but for my mother who I was SO proud of at that moment. Her anger and resentment was momentarily gone, and her feelings came through.

We left after a few more minutes, and as we walked through the cemetery towards the exit, I started to cry. I told my mom how much I appreciated her coming with me to the grave, and how much coming here meant to me. I am so thankful to Henrietta for giving my mom up, so that she could have a better life, and obviously I would not be here if that had not occurred. This is actually what it all came down to. I tried not to over-react, as I wanted my mom to stay calm and relaxed about what just happened. We returned to the hotel and after lunch, made plans to head to the Town Hall.

We made inquiries about the city bus that would take us to the Town Hall to meet my Councillor friend. Once we arrived at the town hall she introduced us to the Mayor of South Shields, who proceeded to give us a back stage tour of the historical Town Hall. We got to see a big leather bound book that holds the signatures of visitors. We signed our names just a few pages past the page that Lady Diana signed from several years back!! We had tea with the Mayor in the Mayor's office and were able to see the Council Chambers.

It was really interesting and very cool that we got to do this. They were so welcoming and happy that my mom had returned to visit her place of birth.

Wherever we went, people would overhear our obviously 'non-English accents', and would lean over and ask, "What brought you to South Shields? - nobody comes here!" Any time we mentioned to anyone that my mom was born in South Shields, people would hug her, kiss her and tell her how happy they were to see her!

After the tour of the Town Hall, we hailed a taxi and headed to John and Marjorie's. My mom was very unsure about going there, and of course, I assured her that if she didn't feel comfortable with it, I would not pressure her to go. But knowing her like I do, I knew she wouldn't want to sit in the hotel wondering what they were like, so she agreed to come and meet them. The taxi dropped us off in front of their terrace house, and they came out to greet us with open arms and hugs.

We sat together in their living room and talked. I asked LOTS of questions while they served us tea, sandwiches and muffins. When I inquired about any photographs, they gave us a whole photo album full of labeled pictures of the WHOLE family!!! It is a treasure!!!!! I was so blown away, that not only did we get to see pictures of my mom's mother, but we got to take the photo album home with us. I was hoping to see photos of Henrietta as a young woman, but there were none.

We learned a lot of details about the circumstances of the family, including a few amazing stories. For example, they told us that Henrietta always talked about my mom. She had a copy of a photograph of my mother from when she graduated from Nursing School. She apparently would show this photo to anyone she knew and tell them that she had a daughter in Toronto that was a nurse. Now, keep in mind, that Henrietta had not seen my mother since she was 8 years old. We figure that she got a copy of the photograph from The Fairbridge Society, because my mom had sent them a copy of the newspaper clipping with the photo of the graduating class, and they must have given Henrietta a copy of it. Apparently she treasured that photo. I asked if they still had the photo, but they didn't.

The family certainly felt that Henrietta was a loving, kind, gentle person. She wore her grey hair in a bun and was very short in stature. She loved babies. She was heartbroken to give her children away, but they were VERY poor and she could not manage. I think I always knew this was the case, and have always been able to imagine that given the historical context of the time such as the war and poverty, I have been able to understand her motivations.

John's brother, Beatrice's first son, David also joined us for lunch, and he had such a strong Geordie accent, that it was very difficult to understand him. He and John joked around with each other a lot, and answered my questions. I liked them very much but my mom and I both noticed that nobody really had any questions for her. They never inquired about her life or her feelings about being given up.

We also met John's daughter, Beatrice's grand daughter, Kathryn, who announced that she was pregnant with her second child. She brought along her daughter, Amelia who was sweet. We discussed the coincidence that we shared the same name and the same spelling of our name. This to me was one of many coincidences. I had been communicating with Kathryn on Facebook before our trip, so it was nice to finally meet her. She was also very helpful in connecting me with her father for this trip.

When David stood up to go, we asked him if would be possible for him to possibly drive us to Maxwell Street, which is where my mom lived when she was 8 years old. It was not far from John and Marjorie's house. He happily drove us there, and allowed us to get out of the car and wander down the street and snap a couple of pictures. Maxwell Street was now a commercial and industrial street with mostly businesses. Any homes had since been torn down. My mom didn't really remember anything about the street, but it was still neat to be there.

David drove us back to our hotel, at which time, we ordered a cup of tea, sat on the sunny, outdoor patio and recounted the events of the day.

I was still recovering from hearing about Henrietta having a photograph of my mom as a nurse. I said to my mom, " Do you realize that we learned that she never forgot about you and loved you and was proud to tell people you were a nurse???" Her response was a bit angry, especially at the thought that someone gave her mother a photograph without her permission. Her feelings of course, were understandable. I will always hold dear to me the fact that my mother was loved and remembered. Like most children given up for adoption, I am sure she wondered if her family

ever thought about her. Now she knew that her mother never forgot her and always loved her. For me it was an epic moment. I understand how hurt my mom has been by the circumstances of her life and how she can't just forget about it. For me, it made the trip worthwhile to know that she came from family that seemed to have good values and were kind. That is how I summed up our re-connecting with the family.

We enjoyed our tea in the English sunshine. It was a really big day. Our heads were spinning from all the things we saw and learned. I think I was still stunned to actually meet people who knew my mother's mother, and her sister Beatrice. They were never real people until now.

That night, we went to the pub for a drink. Afterwards, we planned to take a taxi or a bus down to the beach and seafront. A man at the next table who overheard us and noticed our Canadian accents, offered to drive us there! We were so thrilled. He left his wife at the table and took us down to the beach in his little car. He was so friendly and interested in why we were visiting South Shields. After explaining that my mom had been born here, he was so kind and wished us well. We were so appreciative! We walked along the newly renovated seafront, and looked at the sea. It was where my mother had played and ridden a pony as a young girl. She didn't have strong memories of that time, but vague ones. Again, we were so lucky to have good weather, as we walked for a long time, into the South Marine Park and up Ocean Road. We planned to come back for some Indian food, which South Shields was known for.

The next day we took a bus to the main depot in South Shields, and transferred to a bus that would take us to the Marsden Bay. I had seen so many pictures of the beautiful Marsden Rock and the beach at Marsden. It was just a short bus ride outside of South Shields. This is a place where people go to see the beautiful views of the sea and you can walk on the beach where there are large rock formations. The walk down the steps was very steep so my mom agreed to wait for me while I went down to take a look. It was a beautiful but windy day. I was one of possibly five people on the whole beach and it was so nice to put my hand in the water, collect some sand and rocks and take pictures. There were hundreds of sea gulls making nests in the cliff bank, and the noise of the birds was quite loud. I took a short video of the beach. I wondered if my mom had ever been here as a child.

Since returning from our trip, the photograph I took of the beach that day now hangs over the fireplace in my house.

We hopped back on the city bus that took us back to Ocean Road, downtown South Shields. We were hungry for lunch, and being our last day, I was keen to try some curry from one of South Shield's famous Indian Restaurants. It was around 2:30 in the afternoon, so strangely, most of the restaurants were closed until dinner time.

The only place we could find open, was Coleman's. I had read about Coleman's as being famous for its fish and chips. We decided to go inside to eat. Well… we are still talking about how good that plate of fish and chips was! There is a sign on the wall inside the restaurant that stated the name and number of the fish boat our fish came from and when it was caught. The fish was fresh, the chips were thick and crispy and the mushy peas were to DIE for. It was delicious. And VERY busy.

This was obviously the place to go for Fish and Chips in South Shields.

We wandered back down to the beach for one last look, and I had to snap a photograph of the iconic Groyne - the lighthouse at the end of the pier in South Shields. Its red and white paint make it a popular landmark. I was so happy with all the things were were able to see and do while here. We found family, visited graves, touched the sea, ate Fish and Chips, met lovely people, and thoroughly enjoyed ourselves.

We spent our last night at the Pub, watching Chelsea beat Manchester in football (soccer). The crowd in the pub was wild and it was really busy. It was fun to be doing what the locals do.

We packed our suitcases in preparation for our flight home from Newcastle the next morning. We arranged for a taxi the night before our departure so we would be all ready to go. Our flight was early, and we would have to change planes at Heathrow, in London. It was a long day returning home, and by the time we got in the door, it was around 2:30am Toronto time. I spent the night in Oakville and Kevin picked me up to take me home to Goderich the next morning. We were tired but happy. Our trip had been a true success.

Since returning home, I have worked more extensively on my mom's family tree. I have been able to trace the Hoult family all the way back to 1642. I also worked hard to locate my mom's brother John and sister Mary who were given up and sent to live in Australia. I did a lot of research on the internet, and was able to find Mary Donnelly Kenworthy still listed in the phone book, near Fremantle, in Coolbellup, Western Australia. I could find no death record for her so I assumed she must be still living.

With my mom's blessing, I wrote her a letter telling her that I was doing family research having just returned from England. In the meantime, I was able to find a death record for John, who died in his hometown not far from Mary in 2010. His wife Jenny had also passed away.

It was about 3 months later, that I received a response to my letter to Mary. Her grandson Chad and his wife Hannah wrote me a letter, on behalf of Mary, saying how happy she was to hear from me and to find my mom again! She was over the moon. Mary was 84 years old and in poor health. She lost her husband Roland several years ago, and had two sons, Kevin and Jeffrey. They illustrated a family tree of their family for me so I would know who was who. Then I found her grandson Chad on Facebook and began chatting with him. We sent pictures back and forth and talked to each other about his grandmother and my mother. He loved his grandmother so much and he spent a lot of time with her. Chad and Hannah have two daughters. Chad and I shared a lot of information about Fairbridge and he was able to locate many photographs of Mary when she was living at Fairbridge. He found photos of Mary with my mom from her visit in 1959.

Through Chad, I then connected with Nicole, who is my mom's brother John's grand-daughter. She never knew about her grandfather's family at all! She was so excited to learn that there was more family - especially in Canada. It is apparent that John told his family half-truths to shield them from knowing the truth about his past. There is such a theme of shame with child migrants, and here is a perfect example of that. He told his family that he was from Ireland. He mentioned he had a sister Evelyn, but said she lived in Australia. They never searched for her, but he never wanted them to. I also learned that John's wife, Jenny was also a Fairbridge girl, they met at the Pinjarra Farm School. Jenny and Mary were best friends. Jenny came from Scotland.

I have since Skyped with Nicole and met her whole family on the computer. Her father Mark was very close to his father, John, and he is so happy to have met family too. The family in Australia is fairly close knit. John and Mary were very close their whole lives, only living a few miles away from each other. They both lived in the same homes for years and years. They remembered meeting my mom in 1959, and now we all wish they had kept in touch. The Australian cousins feel that they have missed out on getting to know their Canadian connections. Nicole and Chad have both sent away for their Grandparent's Fairbridge files, so it will be interesting to see what we learn from those. I have sent them both copies of my extensive family tree. It is really unbelievable to think what we have learned about this family only in the past two years.

I have also just recently sent and received a letter from Caroline Widmer, Beatrice's daughter, who lives in Switzerland. I was able to find her address and I sent her a long letter asking if she had any further information or photographs of Lottie and the family. She wrote me a lovely letter and mostly detailed how Lottie kept Beatrice very close to her most of the time because she was afraid to be alone. She always said she hoped that her children would come back to her one day and forgive her for giving them up. She sent along a photograph of her family.

Six months after making contact with my Mom's sister Mary, she passed away in November 2015.

Previous to the last two years, we knew next to nothing about my mom's family. At this point, I can be fairly certain that hard times and war years took their toll on this family. Living in northeast England, in a town on the River Tyne, made South Shields a target during the war. Families were divided or killed and parents were encouraged to make difficult choices for the well being of their children. Many children were evacuated temporarily to safer locations, while others, like my mom and her siblings, were sent away permanently. You can only wonder what kind of pressure was put on these parents to take such a drastic measure. I have learned that some organizations like Fairbridge had social workers that were told to pressure parents, by praying on their vulnerability. They may have even been promised compensation for giving their children up. My mother's mother often referred to the fact that she "was not paid a cent" for giving her children to Fairbridge. These remarks painted her in a very negative light, but after learning about the tactics used to obtain healthy, intelligent children, it makes me wonder.

My mother was a perfect example of the kind of children Fairbridge wanted. They wanted children who would grow up in a new country, contribute to the building of that commonwealth country, and relieve England of them being a burden. In her case, she was one of the luckiest ones. While she suffered separation from family and was forced to live in large, loveless orphan homes, I do not believe she suffered physical abuse. She was educated well. She was taken in by a loving, supportive family and went on to have a happy, fulfilling life.

As much as I learn about this terrible time in British history, I cannot help but think and be saddened by the things my mom and her siblings had to endure on their journey to their new countries. I am saddened to think of all the families that were divided. Not only were the children missing their parents, but the parents must have suffered immensely to give their children away. Many children were told their parents had died, when in fact they often hadn't.

We always knew about my mother's family, but until now, didn't know if they survived the war or what happened to them. With the help of the internet and social media, the ability to trace genealogy has become much, much easier. The world does not seem so vast, when we can simply video chat with a relative half way around the world, or find gravestones in a faraway cemetery.

This journey is not over for me. I still have a lot to discover and learn. And I have some people to get to know. I am so glad my mom is still with me, to help make these discoveries. I am very lucky that she is open and unashamed to share her memories with me and I am so glad she was able to write them down so I could share them with my children.

The Family at The Fairbridge Farm School (2014)

Celebrating my Grandmother's 100th birthday at
Shawnigan Lake, BC - July 2014

Where my mom lived before coming to Canada -
Maxwell Street in the 1930's

Passenger list of mom's emigration to Canada

Evelyn on the far right - at Fairbridge Farm School

My Mom's Mother
Henrietta Charlotte Chatman Jackson
Hoult (Donnelly) (McCabe) (Saunders)
(1904-1977)

My Mom's Brother.
John Donnelly (1926-2010)

My Mom's Sister
Beatrice Donnelly (1927-1988)

My Mom's Sister
Mary (1930-2016)

Lost and Found

(Another chapter to the story!)

(2017)

Well….. Fast forward to July 2017. The Aussie's have just left to return home from a whirlwind trip to Canada!

We had a lot of time to make up for! How do you discuss over 70 years of memories in two weeks?

Two families were divided in 1938 - but they weren't divided anymore.

After making initial contact with my mom's sister, Mary's grandson, Chad Kenworthy, he introduced me to his cousin Nicole—my mom's brother, John's granddaughter. It was hard to believe that someone in this world shared my passion for knowledge, the truth and whereabouts of this divided family!

The first time we chatted was online, by video on the computer, and in an instant, an hour flew by—and I knew this was the beginning of something important and life changing.

The dream to meet an actual blood relative - a Donnelly, was becoming a reality. I chatted with Nicole and her family and Chad and his family. Nicole was especially interested in connecting, so we had lots to talk about. She was anxious to know EVERYTHING I had found in my research, and was determined to add to my research with information she could obtain about her grandfather and her grandmother—who were sweethearts from Fairbridge together. We exchanged census info, photographs and birth certificates. We had found each other and we were now on a journey to discover more.

Then something amazing happened…

Mark and "Aunty Eve"

Nicole called me to say that they had booked a trip to Canada!!! Nicole, her brother Pete and their parents, Mark and Meagan were going to come to Canada to meet my mom and my family! The date was set for August 2, 2017! They would be staying in Canada for two weeks!

I held onto this information for a while until I could wrap my head around it and present it to my mom. Would she be happy to meet them? This crazy idea I had to research this tree was really starting to catch up with me - and become more real than I had ever imagined!

It is a strange feeling to know that I would be meeting flesh and blood family, and having them stay at my home, and meet my mom—who may or may not like this idea very much. What if they weren't nice? What if we didn't get along?

They planned to arrive in Toronto, and stay near the airport for a few days while they visited my mom in Oakville. I had to tell her that her Donnelly clan was coming to meet us and hoped that she would be happy and open to it. I telephoned my mom and said, "Guess who is coming to Canada?" I told her that they were coming here for a holiday and that it would be nice for us to meet. She was quite happy and as the time of their visit got closer, my mom was visibly more and more excited. She planned to have them to her place for lunch, maybe go for a walk to the harbour and chat and get to know each other. We were not nervous and slept well the night before their arrival. Cameron and I had come to Oakville the night before, but Meagan and Kevin stayed home as they had to work.

The Donnelly's and us in Oakville

They arrived in Toronto, and slept a bit before venturing into Oakville to finally meet. This was the moment I had waited my entire life for. This was the culmination of countless hours spent on the internet combing for clues about the Donnelly family who were sent to Pinjarra. I knew they were still in the area in the 1950's but honestly, didn't know how or where to look. I knew I had relatives in Australia, and it was hard to realize that my cousins were not little children, they were grown adults, who could have relocated or passed away.

Anyway, here we were. I was about to meet actual flesh and blood Donnelly's for the first time.

Niagara Falls, Ontario

We felt an instant connection. A bond that you can't describe. There was instant comfort, no nerves and no awkwardness. They were warm, friendly, good people who were fun to be with! We talked, walked, ate lunch and took lots of photos. Mark, John Donnelly's son, called my mom, "Aunty" and kissed her and hugged her. I wasn't sure how my mom would react to this attention, but she loved it. She really did. She took it all in and was excited to see them the next day for a trip to Niagara Falls.

The Aussie's loved Niagara Falls. We took lots of photos, they bought souvenirs and we ended the day with a great dinner by the lake in Oakville. The next day, they would say goodbye to my mom before we all headed to Toronto, to see a Blue Jays game and see the sights of the city.

We took the train to Toronto, and enjoyed people watching before the Ball Game started. Mark and Pete bought jerseys with "Donnelly" on them and Pete bought a signed baseball for a buddy back home. The game was great and afterwards, we ate at a restaurant before heading back to Oakville. We all had a fun time and continued to feel very comfortable with one another.

The following morning, we all drove to Goderich, where the Aussies would spend another week. Before they arrived, I had arranged for them to stay at our friends home, who had graciously offered their place as they would be away on a holiday themselves. This house was the home of our good friends, Mike Murdoch and Teresa Donnelly —so they got to stay at the "Donnelly House". It is an absolutely gorgeous grand Victorian home and upon arrival to it, the Aussies were stunned. The house had a gorgeous pool, but they never once used it as it was too cold for them! (even though it was over 80 degrees!)

We enjoyed showing them around Goderich, the beach, the museum and having dinners together on the patio. We had such a nice time together and we were dreading saying goodbye. One of the things that we did was go through all of the research that I did on my mom and her Fairbridge experience. I showed them the family trees that I created, and showed them document after document about the family. At one point, Mark was very overwhelmed emotionally and he had to take a break to be able to digest all of this information. They knew almost nothing about the circumstances that led to our parents being given up to Fairbridge and being migrated to Australia and Canada.

The night before the Aussie's left for home, we lit firecrackers in a vacant field to mark the occasion. In Australia, firecrackers are only legal ONE night per year, so it was a special treat for them to have some to light. We laughed because they were actually quite disappointing but it was still fun to celebrate this amazing story of reconnection.

It really has been such a journey to not only learn my mother's history but to come full circle and connect lost families again. While my mom never got to see her brother and sister again, we were fulfilled to make connections with their children and for them make the long trip halfway around the world to meet face to face. There are a lot more people to meet, but the one thing we know for sure, is that the bonds of family were undoubtable.

After they left Goderich, I found a hand written letter from Nicole. It was a thank you note but it was so much more than that. It was so special to read the words that mirrored my feelings of how important this meeting was. She and I share a special bond in many ways, because I was able to fill in a lot of holes in her family story, but she filled those holes for me also. The journey is not over yet… but it is off to a wonderful start.

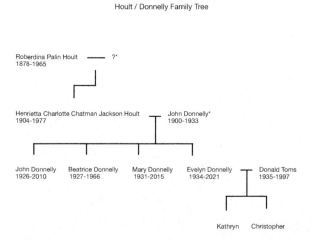

Hoult / Donnelly Family Tree

Roberdina Palin Hoult — ?*
1878-1965

Henrietta Charlotte Chatman Jackson Hoult — John Donnelly*
1904-1977   1900-1933

John Donnelly   Beatrice Donnelly   Mary Donnelly   Evelyn Donnelly — Donald Toms
1926-2010   1927-1966   1931-2015   1934-2021   1935-1997

Kathryn   Christopher

* research conducted following the original publication of this book has brought to light that John Donnelly is not the biological father of Evelyn Donnelly. John Donnelly died 13 months prior to Evelyn's birth, not 1 month as was incorrectly indicated on Fairbridge paperwork. It is believed that Henrietta gave the wrong date of his death to avoid Evelyn's birth appearing to be illegitimate. In 2021, DNA testing was conducted and has resulted in the discovery that her biological father is a man with the last name Spink (full name will not be disclosed) Evelyn's middle name Spink has long been a mystery that is now solved.

* DNA testing has also uncovered the identity of Henrietta's father to be a man with the last name Buchanan.

(as of March 2022)

Printed in Great Britain
by Amazon

41035293R00046